SHITO-RYU KARATE

BY FUMIO DEMURA

WARNING

This book is presented only as a means of preserving a unique aspect of the heritage of the martial arts. Neither Ohara Publications nor the author makes any representation, warranty or guarantee that the techniques described or illustrated in this book will be safe or effective in any self-defense situation or otherwise. You may be injured if you apply or train in the techniques of self-defense illustrated in this book, and neither Ohara Publications nor the author is responsible for any such injury that may result. It is essential that you consult a physician regarding whether or not to attempt any technique described in this book. Specific self-defense responses illustrated in this book may not be justified in any particular situation in view of all of the circumstances or under the applicable federal, state or local law. Neither Ohara Publications nor the author makes any representation or warranty regarding the legality or appropriateness of any technique mentioned in this book.

OHARA PUBLICATIONS, INCORPORATED
SANTA CLARITA, CALIFORNIA

DEDICATION

To Kenwa Mabuni, the founder of Shito-Ryu
and
Ryusho Sakagami, my sensei

Printed in the United States of America
Library of Congress Catalog Card Number: 74-169720
ISBN #0-89750-005-9
Fourteenth printing 1999

PREFACE

Karate, literally translated as "empty hand", is one of the oldest and most effective means of fighting known to man, and is considered to be the ultimate in unarmed self-defense. Karate consists of blocking, shifting, punching, striking and kicking. Although it can be aggressive, it is taught and practiced by most groups as self-defense—countering an attack on the individual.

The layman has often been misled about karate. With few exceptions, erroneous information about the art has stressed the bizarre: board breaking, tile crushing and brick breaking. To add to the confusion, many instructors have capitalized on such feats of strength to display themselves as mystical members of some sort of Oriental secret cult and allow karate to be termed a killer art. It is true that a karateka can smash stacks of tiles with his bare fist and chop through bricks and boards, but such exhibitions are only used to demonstrate the power of a karate blow.

Another misconception of the art is that one must harden or mutilate the hand in order to be effective in karate. Although a zealous student may form callouses on certain parts of the hands and feet by repeated practice, no one has to condition his hands to the extent that they become deformed or impaired.

The essence of karate is speed, and effective application of technique depends on one's ability to properly strike the vulnerable areas of an opponent's body. There is no mystic or secret power to karate, nor are all the movements deadly or dangerous. A well-trained karateka can control his movements to do the amount of damage he desires and can frustrate most attacks without doing grievous harm to his attacker.

Karate movements may seem very odd to the layman, but each movement has been analyzed and geometrically calculated so that whatever the action—a block or punch—, it is the maximum the human body can achieve. One quickly learns that it is not size and strength alone that win; rather, speed and knowledge are the deciding factors in determining who will emerge victorious in physical combat.

For just good exercise, karate ranks among the best because it utilizes all parts of the body and keeps them in tone. Unlike other exercises that are ofttimes boring, karate is always challenging, stimulating and especially purposeful.

True karate is a physical art, a technique of self-defense and a sport. One of its greatest attributes is that anyone, irrespective of size, age or sex, can practice the art according to his own capabilities or in spite of his handicaps.

Fumio Demura

ABOUT THE AUTHOR

Fumio Demura, 5th-dan, was born in Yokohama, Japan. He began his martial arts training during his grammar school years when he studied the art of kendo as a means of building up his strength and improving his health. When his teacher moved from the area, Mr. Demura was relocated to another dojo which taught both karate and kendo. He then studied aikido in high school and, later, judo. While at Nihon University in Tokyo, from which he received a Bachelor of Science Degree in Economics, he developed interest in all the martial arts, including the techniques of such weapons as the bo, sai, tonfa, kama and nunchaku, which he perfected under the tutelage of Mr. Kenshin Taira.

Noted in Japan as an outstanding karateka, Mr. Demura has been honored by martial artists and government officials alike. In 1961 he won the All-Japan Karate Free-Style Tournament and was lauded as one of Japan's top eight players for three consecutive years, from 1961-64. His tournament wins have been numerous, including the East Japan, Shito-Ryu Annual and Kanto District championships. He received the All-Japan Karate Federation President's trophy for outstanding tournament play and has received certificates of recognition from such Japanese Cabinet officials as the Ministers of Education, Finance and Transportation for his outstanding achievements in and contributions to the art of karate.

In response to an invitation by Mr. Dan Ivan, Fumio Demura came to the United States in 1965 to teach Shito-Ryu—one of the

four major systems of karate in the world. He now heads his own dojo in Santa Ana, California and supervises instruction at the University of California at Irvine, Orange Coast College and Fullerton State College. In addition, he is the director of the Japan Karate Federation in the United States and advisor for the Pan-American Karate Association.

Largely as a result of Mr. Demura's unceasing efforts to expand the practice of Shito-Ryu, the system is rapidly gaining a large following throughout the country. Besides his full-time job as an instructor, he has taken on a strenuous demonstration schedule at Japanese Village and Deer Park in Buena Park, California where his exhibitions have become a very important part of the park's attractions.

Although he has only been in the United States six years, Mr. Demura has been honored by such civic organizations as the Junior Chamber of Commerce and the Kiwanis. As a top referee and respected sensei, he has been featured many times in KARATE ILLUSTRATED and BLACK BELT MAGAZINE. In 1969 the Black Belt Hall of Fame paid tribute to his dedication to karate with its coveted Karate Sensei of the Year award.

CONTENTS

THE HISTORY OF SHITO-RYU

Karate originated as a martial art thousands of years ago and was brought to Japan from China, Taiwan and Okinawa. Many of the famous karateka, or **bushi** as they were known in Okinawa, experimented and developed their skills in such provinces as Shuri, Naha and Tomari. But unlike judo and kendo, karate was a secret art, unknown to the general public. There was no fixed system until approximately 1907 when Yastune Itosu of Shuri and Kaneryo Higaonna of Naha—both of whom are regarded today as two of the most influential teachers of Okinawan karate—gained a good following for both of their own special styles. Instructor Itosu taught the Nai-huan-chi form and Higaonna taught Sanchin which was later developed into the present-day GOJU-RYU style by Chojyun Miyagi.

The SHITO-RYU system was devised by Kenwa Mabuni who had studied under both Itosu and Higaonna. Born in 1893, Mabuni was the 17th-generation son of a famous samurai named Onigusuki. Mabuni was keenly aware of the accomplishments of his brave ancestors and, wanting to overcome poor health, began intensive karate training at the age of 13. He also studied weapon

KENWA MABUNI
Founder of the
Shito-Ryu System

techniques of the bo, sai, tonfa, kama and nunchaku from Master Aragaki. By mixing the teaching of Itosu and Higaonna, and, using their initials, he developed a new system and coined it SHITO-RYU. He instructed the secrets of his art to Okinawa's police, constabulary and self-defense forces, and also made frequent visits to Japan prior to 1920 to instruct the art. In 1929 Mabuni made a permanent move to Osaka to teach at universities and police departments. He died in May 1957 at the age of 64, but his system remains one of the four major styles in Japan.

STRIKING POINTS

The striking points are your weapons—the many areas of the body which can be used to stun or disable your assailant. To be effective, however, maximum concentration must be directed to these points at impact.

SEIKEN
(Forefist)

Form your fist properly by rolling the fingertips into the palm and tightening the thumb, as illustrated. By solidifying the hand in this way, you can cause more damage when punching, meanwhile minimizing possible damage to your own hand. The forefinger can be folded in or extended out.

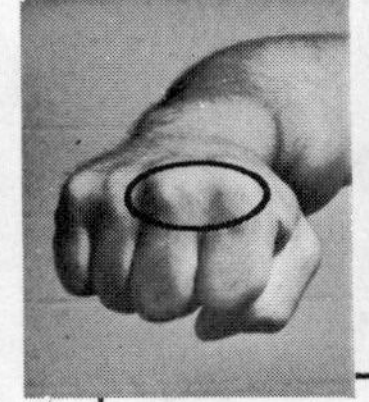

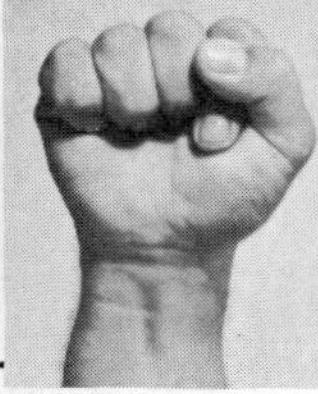

NAKADAKA IPPON KEN
(Middle Finger Knuckle)

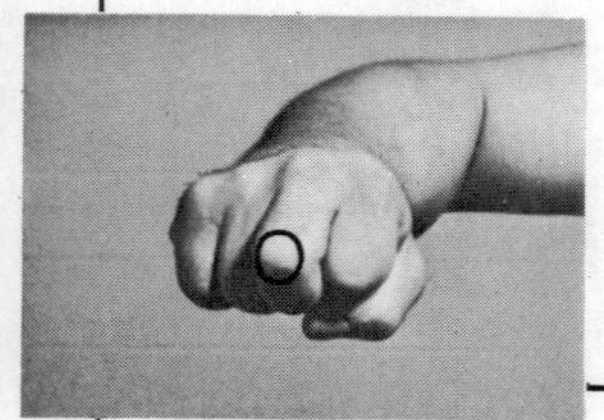

With the middle finger knuckle protruding, you can concentrate your power on a small area such as the eye, temple, throat, solar plexus or a rib.

HITOSASHI IPPON KEN
(Forefinger Knuckle)

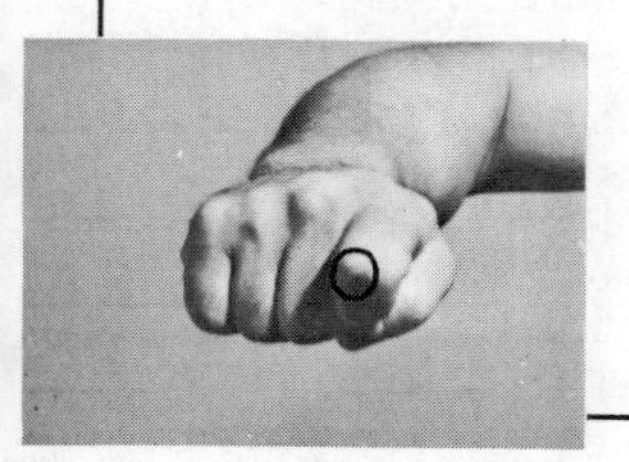

A similar concentration of power on a small area can be effectively gained from the use of the forefinger knuckle.

HIRA KEN
(Knuckle Joints)

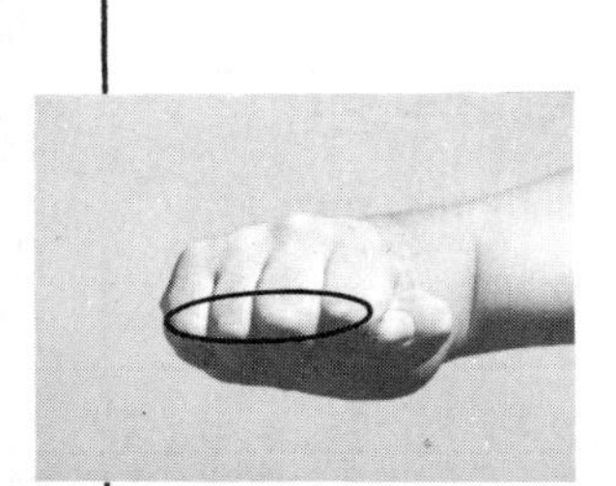

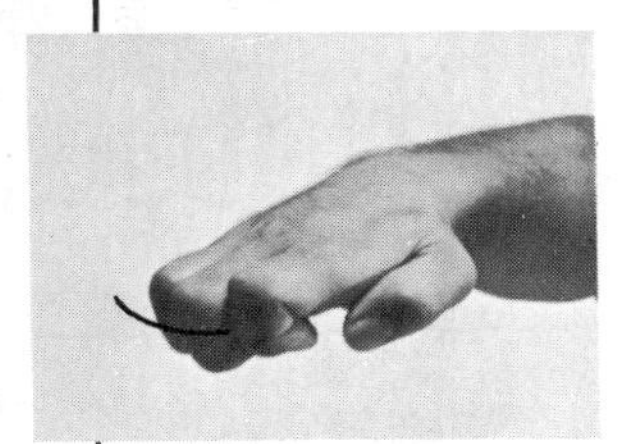

To penetrate crevice areas such as the solar plexus or bridge of the nose, you can either extend the finger knuckles in a stabbing motion (top photo) or swipe with the area immediately below the knuckles (lower photo).

URA KEN
(Back Fist)

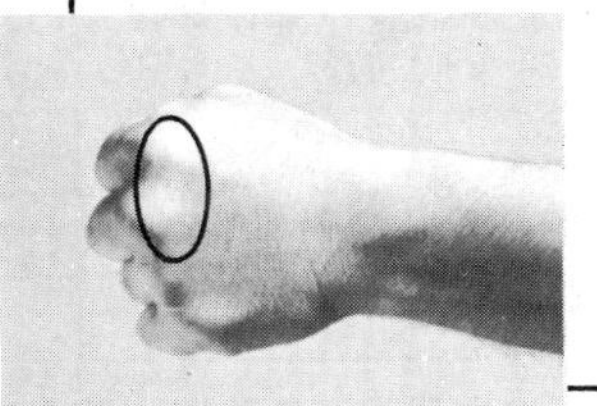

By snapping the elbow into the blow, the back fist is a strong weapon and is especially effective in striking opponents who are standing at your side.

OYAYUBI IPPON KEN
(Thumb Knuckle)

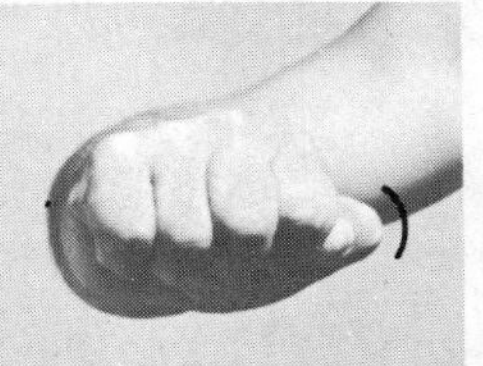

Like most single-knuckle strikes, the thumb knuckle is used to concentrate power in small areas. You may, for instance, execute a circular strike to the temple or a straight uppercut to the chin.

KEN TSUI
(Bottom Fist)

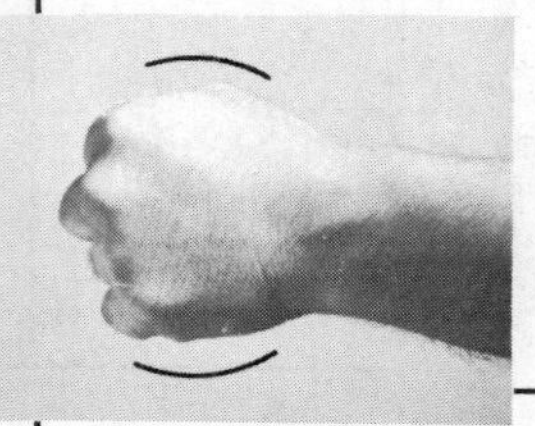

Commonly referred to as a hammer fist, both the top and bottom of the fist can be used. The bottom fist is considered to be a powerful blow and for the beginner is often a stronger defense than punching.

YON HON NUKITE
(Four-Finger Spear)

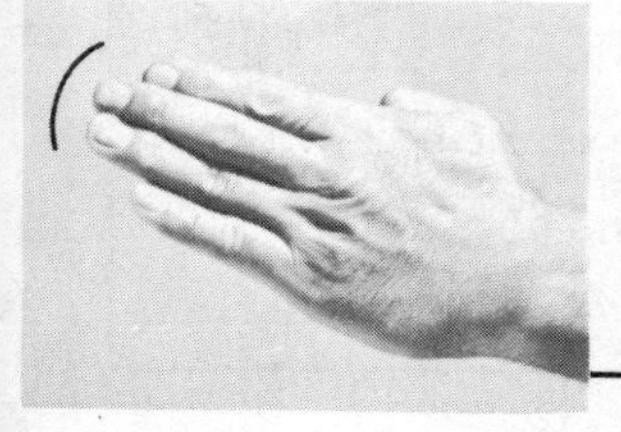

Referred to as a spear hand, the four-finger spear is used to penetrate such crevice areas of the body as the throat and solar plexus, or to stab the eyes.

NI HON NUKITE
(Two-Finger Spear)

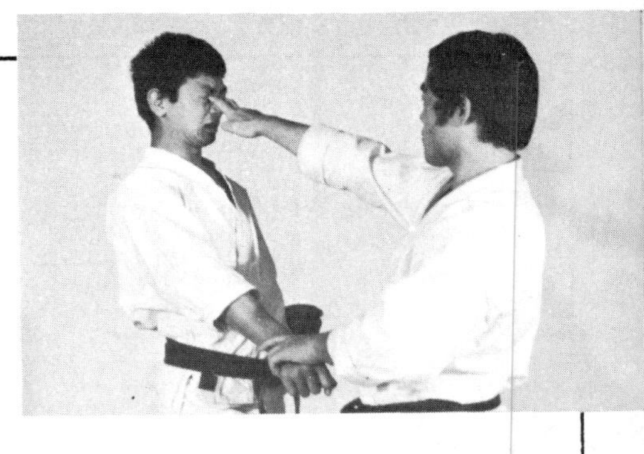

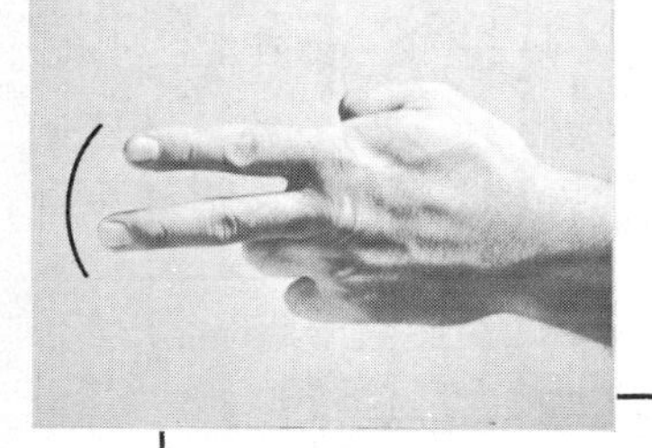

With the fingers spaced like a prong, the two-finger spear is primarily used for eye attacks.

IPPON NUKITE
(One-Finger Spear)

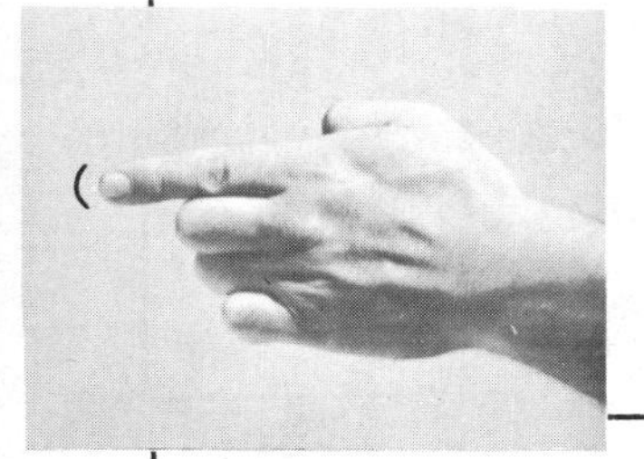

The forefinger attack is directed mainly toward the eyes. On all fingertip attacks, keep the end joints slightly bent to ensure their collapse into a normal fold with excess force.

OYAYUBI
(Thumb)

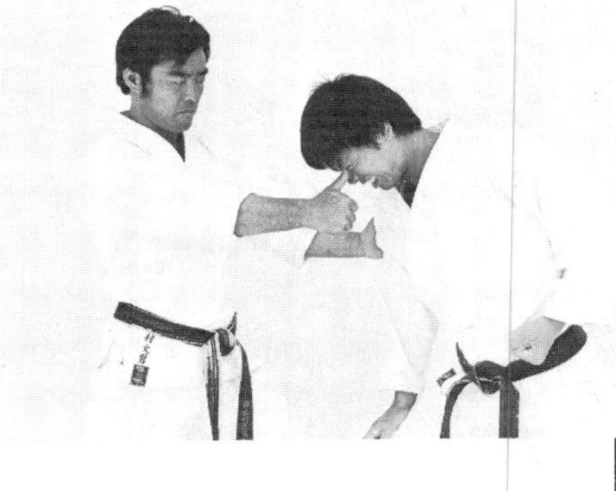

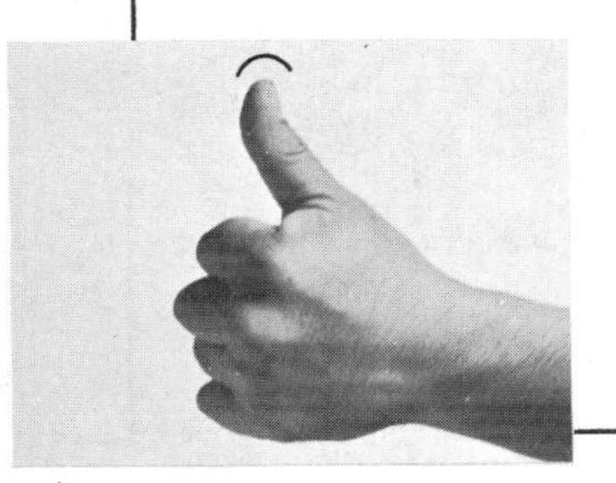

The thumb thrust is used chiefly for gouging.

SHUTO
(Sword or Knife-Hand)

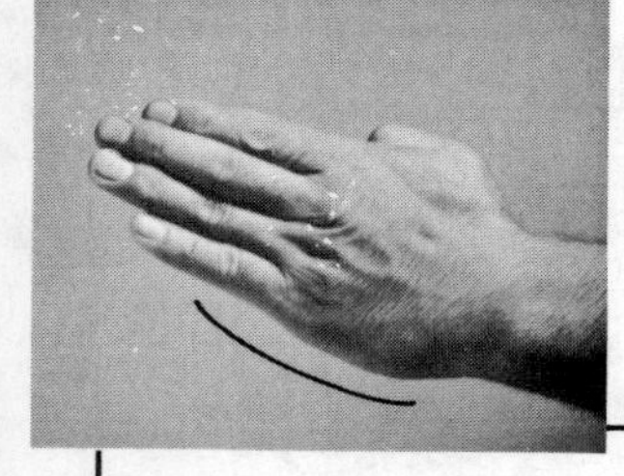

The knife-edge of the hand, which must be rigid and tense, is used for chopping.

SEIRYU TOH
(Palm Edge)

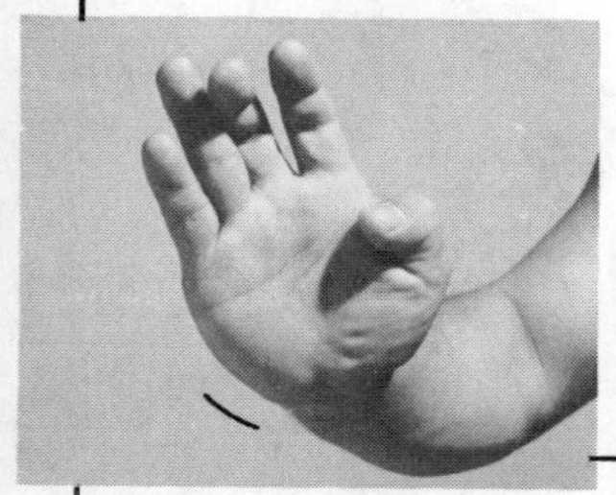

Utilizing a snap of the wrist, strike with the top of the hand, as illustrated. This technique is also known as a form of the Crane.

TEISHO
(Palm Heel)

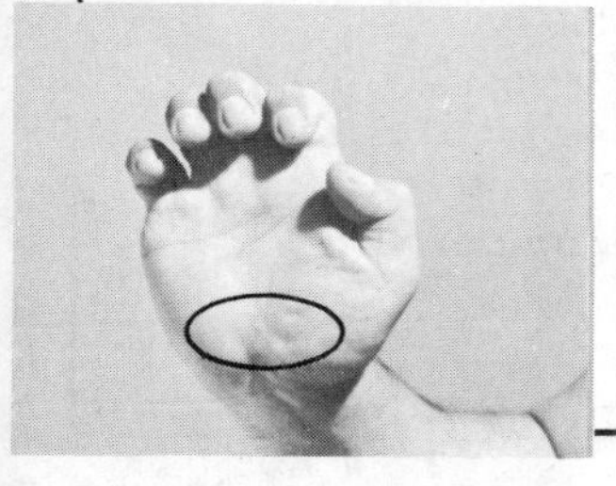

The palm heel uses the entire palm-corner surface to thrust into the target.

KOKEN
(Wrist Joint)

Utilizing a snap of the wrist, strike with the top of the hand, as illustrated. This technique is also known as a form of the Crane.

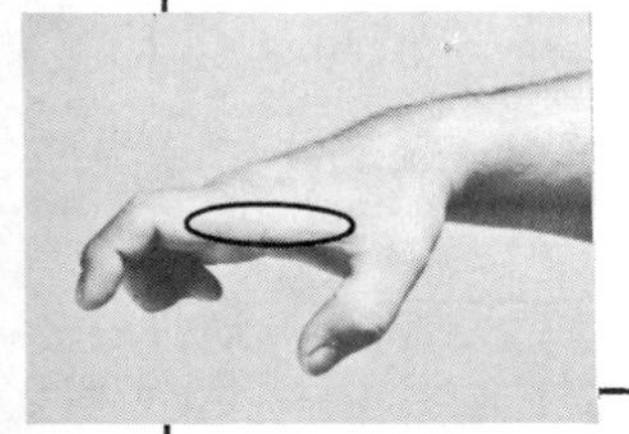

KEIKO
(Joined Fingertips)

With the fingers drawn toward each other in the "chicken's beak", they can be used in a pecking action.

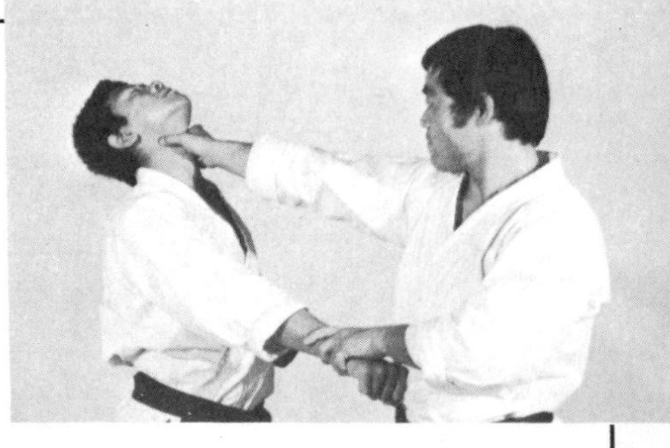

HERABASAMI
(Inside Ridge-Hand)

Also known as a "tiger mouth", the inside ridge-hand is used for strikes to such areas as the throat and up under the nose.

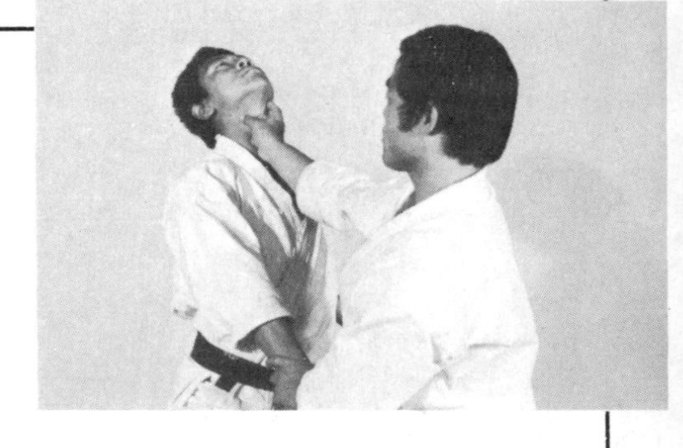

YUBI BASAMI
(Knuckle/Fingertip Strike)

The knuckle of the middle finger can be used to strike the adam's apple as thumb and forefinger claw or grip the throat. This strike can also be used with the eyes as the target.

HIJI
(Elbow Strike)

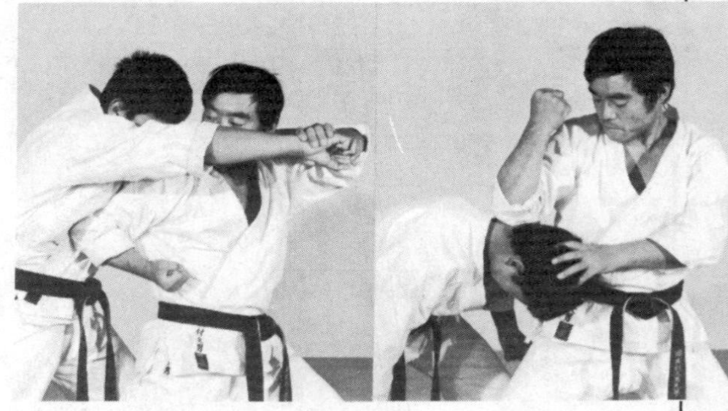

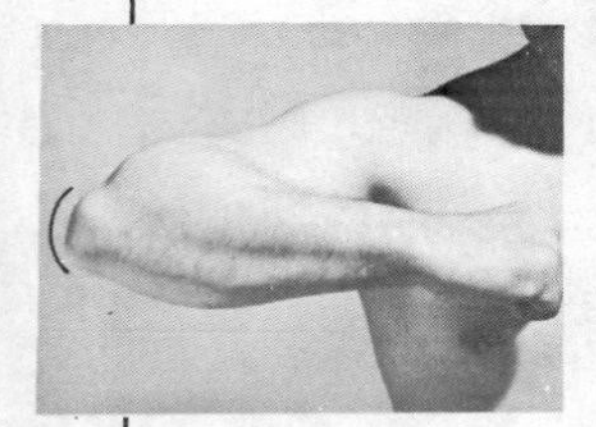

Elbow strikes are especially useful for close-in fighting with blows to the throat, chin, ribs or back of the neck.

HAITO
(Ridge-Hand)

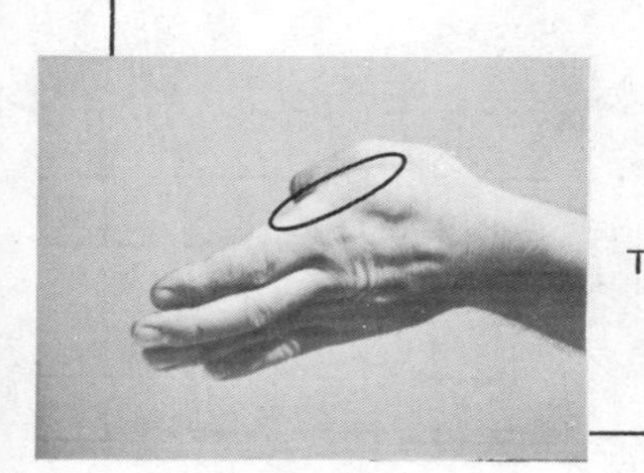

The side of the open hand is used for striking.

HAISHU
(Open Backhand)

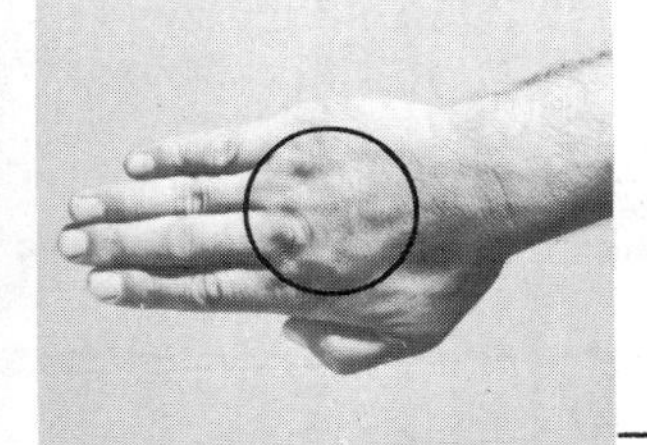

The open backhand is used in the same manner as the closed back fist.

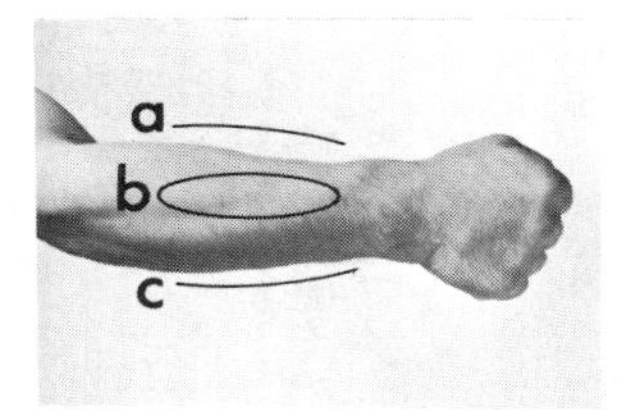

KOTE (Forearm)

The three sections of the forearm—(a) Omote, (b) Hera, and (c) Ura—are used for blocking as well as smashing blows.

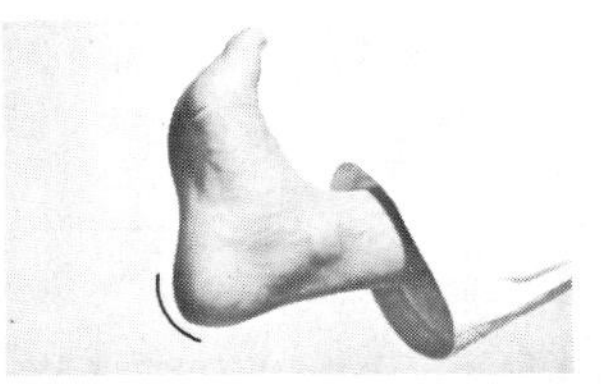

KA-SOKU-TEI (Bottom Heel)

The bottom of the heel is used for front thrust kicks in a similar manner to the front snap except that more hip power must be utilized in a thrusting manner. This portion of the heel is also used in the back kick.

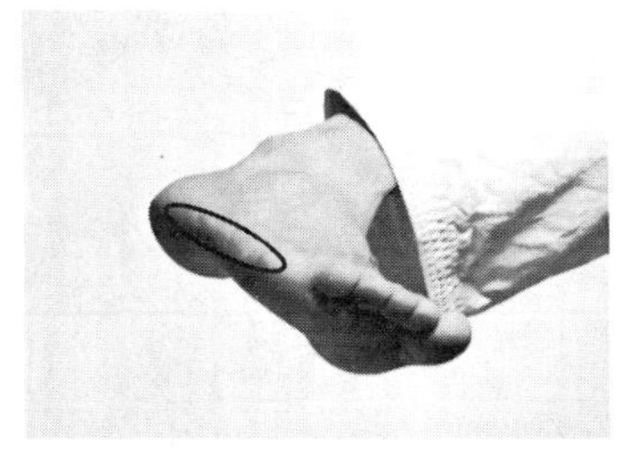

SOKU-TO (Edge of Foot)

The side edge of the foot is used in both a snapping and thrusting manner for the side kick.

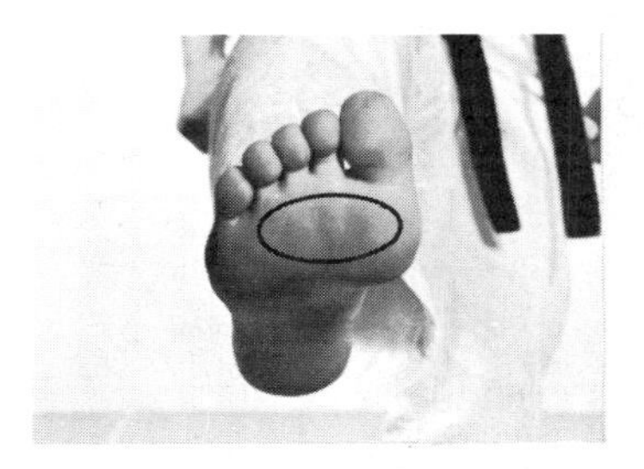

JO-SOKU-TEI (Ball of Foot)

Use the ball of your foot for a front snap kick when you are barefoot.

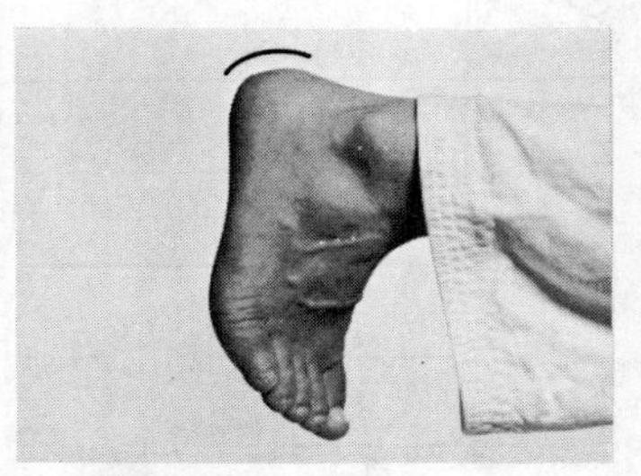

USHIRO-KAKA-TO
(Backside of Heel)

In a back snap kick or hook-type kick, the back side of the heel makes contact with the target.

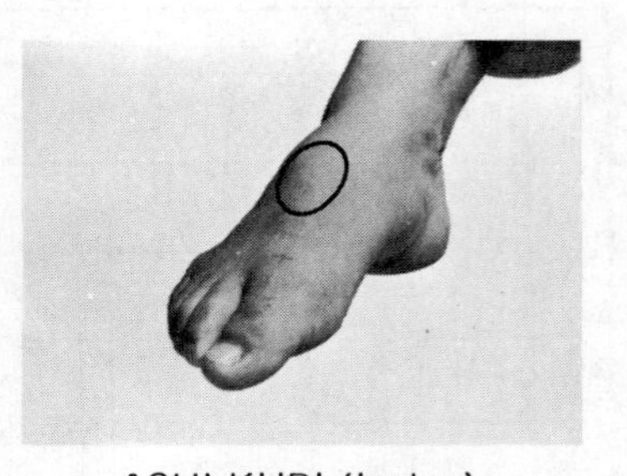

ASHI-KUBI (Instep)

The instep can be used for forward-type kicks and roundhouse kicks.

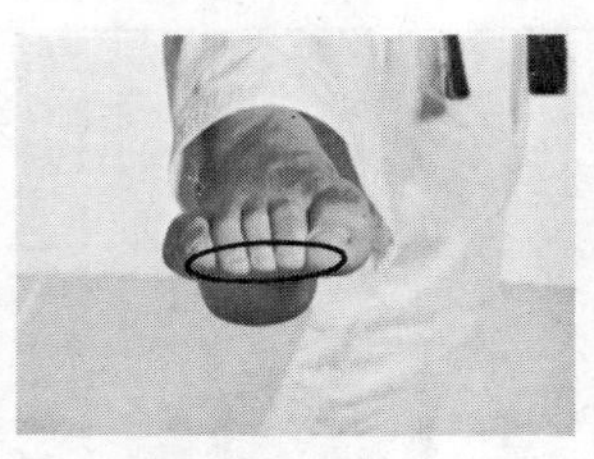

TSUMA-SAKI (Tip of Toes)

Forward kicks sometimes use the tips of the toes. It must be noted that Asians, who are often barefoot, have more than the normal amount of strength in their toes.

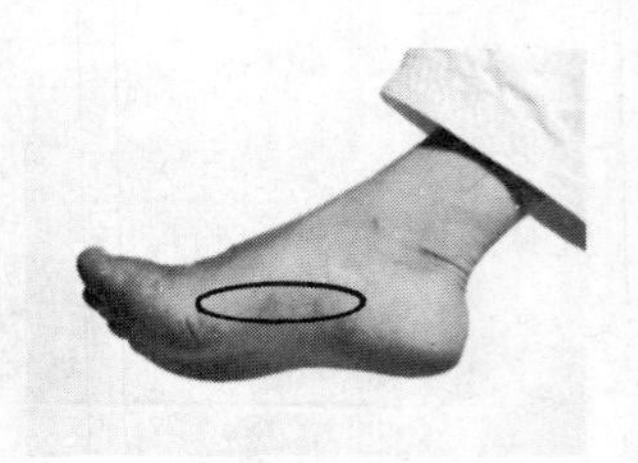

UCHI-SOKU-TO
(Inside Edge of Foot)

The inside edge of the foot is used for stomping the instep and for sweeps.

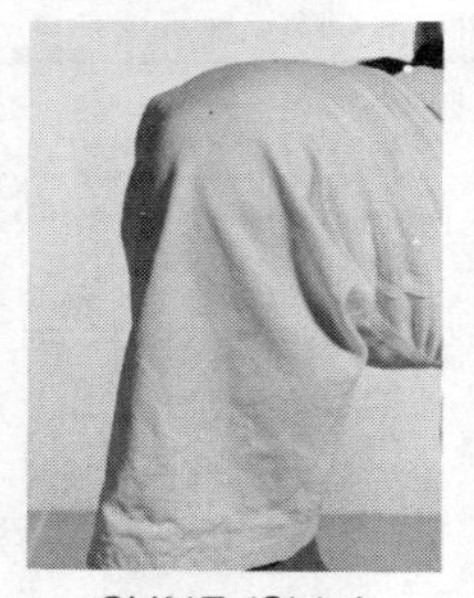

SUNE (Shin)

The shin area is used for blocking against kicks.

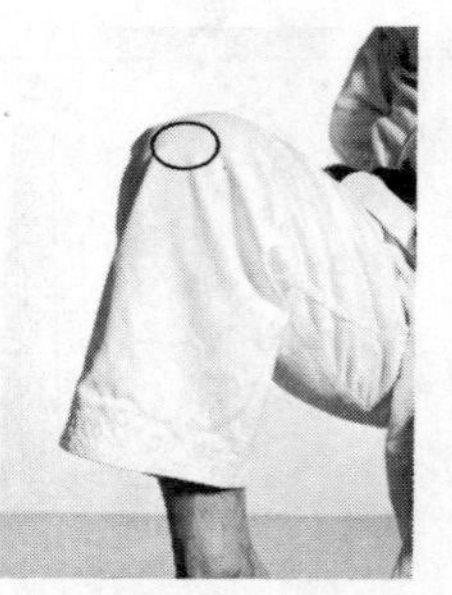

HIZA (Knee)

The knee is an excellent weapon for close-in fighting.

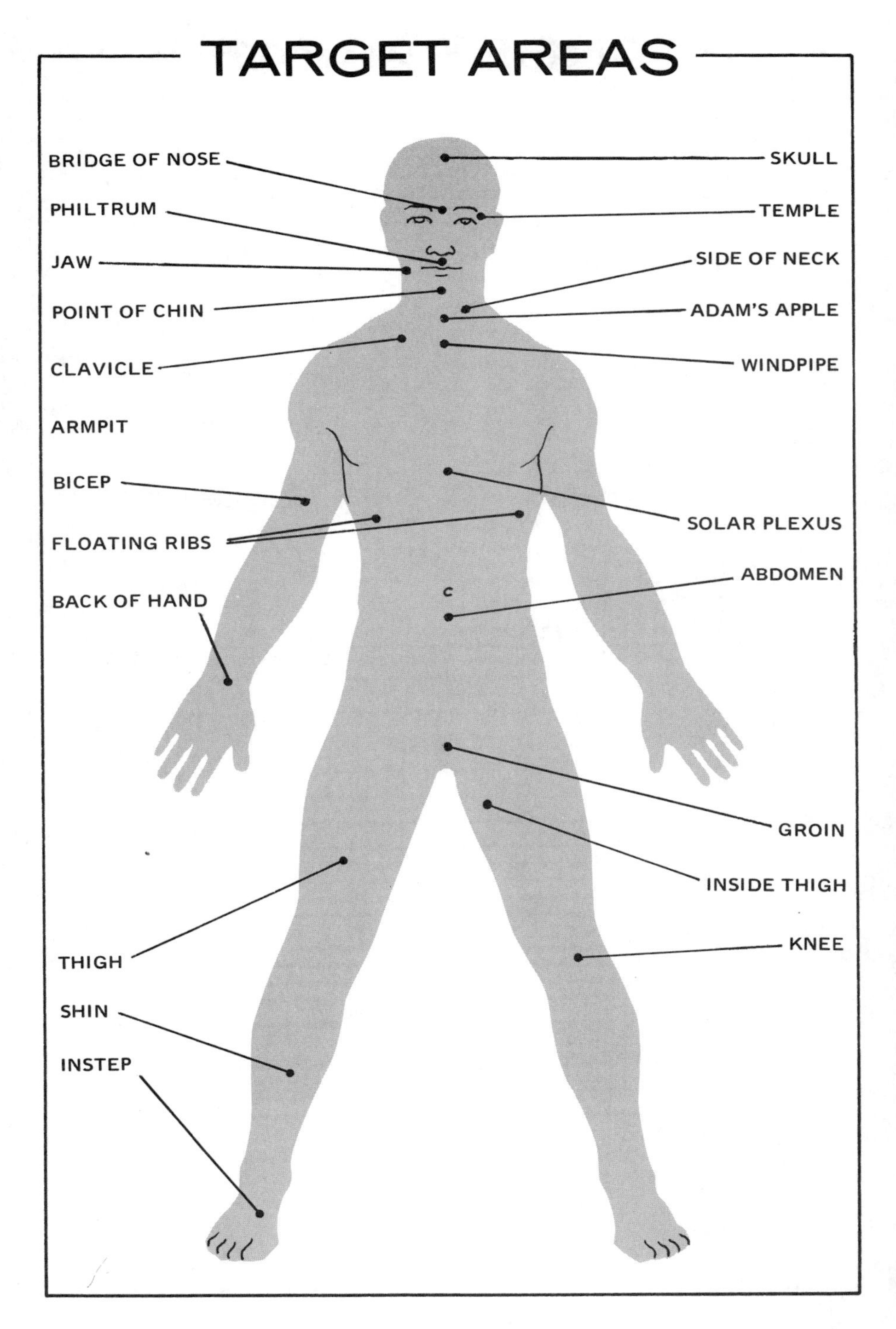
TARGET AREAS
BRIDGE OF NOSE
PHILTRUM
JAW
POINT OF CHIN
CLAVICLE
ARMPIT
BICEP
FLOATING RIBS
BACK OF HAND
THIGH
SHIN
INSTEP
SKULL
TEMPLE
SIDE OF NECK
ADAM'S APPLE
WINDPIPE
SOLAR PLEXUS
ABDOMEN
GROIN
INSIDE THIGH
KNEE

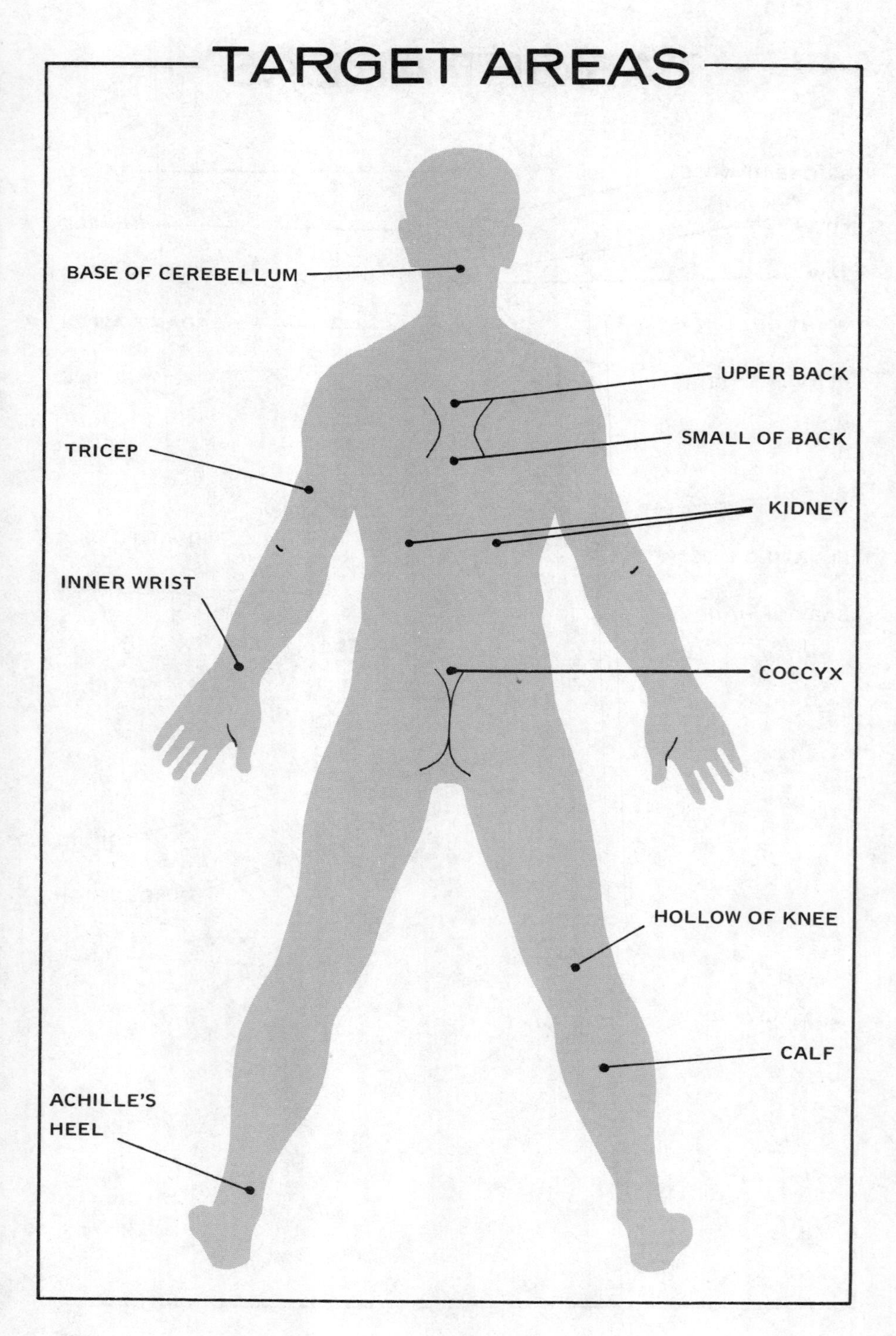
TARGET AREAS
BASE OF CEREBELLUM
UPPER BACK
SMALL OF BACK
TRICEP
KIDNEY
INNER WRIST
COCCYX
HOLLOW OF KNEE
CALF
ACHILLE'S
HEEL

STANDING POSITIONS

The stance is more than just standing. One must concentrate primarily on achieving a relaxed body, free of tension, to exert maximum stability, speed and control. Do not force the stance or use unnecessary energy. Hip movement must be coordinated with balance in order to flow smoothly into the next move.

HEISOKU DACHI

A ready position in which your feet are together and arms are at your sides. Also, prepare to bow from this position.

MUSUBE DACHI

A ready position in which your heels are together, toes pointed outward, and your hands are crossed in front of your body. Some kata start from this position.

HEIKO DACHI

A natural position in which your feet are spread slightly apart, toes pointed forward, and your clenched fists are held in front of and away from your body. This position is most commonly used prior to practicing basic sparring.

SOTO HACHIJI DACHI

A natural position, similar to heiko-dachi, except the toes are pointed outward.

"T" DACHI

A natural ready position in which one of your feet is pointed forward and the other to the side, in a T formation. One arm, with clenched fist pointed downward, is extended over the forward foot while the other clenched fist is held, palm up, at waist level.

"V" DACHI

A natural ready position, similar to "T" dachi, except the back foot is angled forward in a V formation.

VARIATION

NAI FAN CHIN DACHI

A straddle leg, or horse, stance in which your legs are spread wide apart from a deep knee bend so that they are wider than the shoulders, and your toes are pointed forward. Clenched fists are held out to their sides. This position is used to brace the body against side attacks, and also for side-stepping to avoid frontal attacks.

VARIATION

HIKO DACHI

A straddle leg stance similar to the nai-fan-chin-dachi except the toes are pointed outward in a more relaxed manner.

VARIATION

NEKO ASHI DACHI

A cat stance in which most of your weight is placed on the back leg while the front leg rests lightly on the ball of the foot, knees bent. Your clenched fists are held out to the sides.

VARIATION

KOKUTSU DACHI

A back stance in which your forward knee is bent and the other leg fully extended, toes pointed to the side. One clenched fist is placed at your waist on the forward foot side while the other fist is extended downward and aligned with the other leg. Most of your weight is distributed over the back leg. This position is mainly used in a defensive or evasive tactic.

VARIATION

SAGIASHI DACHI

A one-leg, or crane, stance in which you stand on one leg which is slightly bent with toes pointed outward, and raise the other leg to prepare to kick. One arm, fist clenched, is extended to block while the other clenched fist is held at your waist. This position is used to defend or kick.

VARIATION

SANCHIN DACHI

An inside, tensed stance in which your legs are spread slightly apart, toes pointed inward. Your clenched fists are extended downward and slightly outward. This position is used for dynamic tension practice and close-in fighting.

ZENKUTSU DACHI

A forward stance in which your forward leg is bent at the knee and the other leg extended backward. Arms are extended downward and slightly outward with fists clenched. This position is primarily used to attack with the back leg since it has so much thrusting power.

KOSA DACHI

A crossed-leg stance in which your legs and arms cross each other. When your right leg crosses your left, you must also cross your right arm over your left, both fists clenched. Your front foot should be planted flat on the floor while your back foot rests only on the toes. This position is usually used as a recovery from a jump but can also be used as a maneuvering tactic for a kick with the "hidden foot", or to pivot evasively.

HAND TECHNIQUES

One must relax in order to punch, hit or kick. Tensing up prior to punching is not only unnecessary, but a waste of your strength as well. The move should be executed with smoothness and speed until the moment of contact when the power of the entire body—called kime, or focus—is applied to enforce the blow.

TSUKI

(Punch)

(1) Assume a normal ready position with your right clenched fist on your hip and your left arm extended, palm down, in a punching position. (2) Retract your left hand to your hip as you punch out with the right in a turning corkscrew action. (3) Your right hand should be fully extended and your left at the hip. By retracting your hand swiftly, you can create more speed and power in your punch.

1

URAKEN

(Backhand)

(1) Assume a ready position with your left clenched fist on your hip and your right arm cocked at the elbow, the elbow facing outward, with the fist turned downward and your face toward the target. (2) Snap your hand in a straight, overhand motion until your arm is (3) fully extended. Snap your arm back in the same way you extended it. (Note: As long as the striking surface remains the same, you can also strike straight across or in an underarm motion, in addition to the overhand snap shown.)

1

2
3
2
3

SHUTO UCHI

(Chop)

(1) From a ready position, extend your left hand outward, and position your right chopping hand near the right ear, palm outward. (2) Chop in a circular motion as you retract your left hand to the left hip. (3) Complete the movement with the palm facing upward. Your left clenched fist should be on the hip in a ready punch position.

GYAKU SHUTO

(Reverse Chop)

(1) Prepare the backhanded chop with your right hand drawn across your body—palm facing toward the left ear—and the left hand extended outward, palm down. (2) Chop outward, your elbow pointing down, as you retract your left hand to your hip. (3) The movement is completed when the right palm faces down and the left clenched fist is on your hip.

2
3
2
3

MOROTE ZUKI

(U-Punch)

(1) Assume a ready position with both clenched fists on your hips. Simultaneously propel your right hand upward to punch as the left goes downward. (3) The target area for the right hand is the face and for the left hand, the stomach.

HEIKO ZUKI

(Double Punch)

(1) Assume a ready position with both fists on your hips. (2) Simultaneously punch forward with both hands in a corkscrew manner. (3) Both fists must be fully extended, palm down, to complete the double punch.

2
3
2
3

FURI ZUKI

(Flare Punch)

(1) Assume a ready position with your right fist clenched at your hip and your left arm, fist clenched, extended out. (2) Swing or flare the right elbow out, propelling your fist forward. (3) Extend the fist out in a circular motion, hitting with the first two knuckles, palm facing slightly outward.

KAGI ZUKI

(Hook Punch)

(1) Assume a ready position with your clenched right fist at your hip and your left arm extended, fist clenched and palm down. Your eyes should be directed toward the left. (2) Bring your right hand across your body in a punching motion as you begin to retract your left hand to your hip. (3) Hook the right-hand punch across your body, forming a 90-degree angle, and draw the left hand back to the hip.

2
3
2
3

ELBOW TECHNIQUES

YOKO HIJI ATE

(Side Elbow Strike)

Cross your right hand over your extended left arm at shoulder level. Keeping your right fist as close to your body as possible, snap your elbow out to the right, retracting your left clenched fist, palm up, to the hip.

MAWASHI HIJI ATE

(Circular Elbow Strike)

With your right fist clenched, palm up, at the hip and your left arm extended straight out from the body, circle the right elbow to the front until the fist faces toward the body, palm down. Simultaneously return your left hand, fist clenched and palm up, to the hip.

TATE HIJI ATE

(Upward Elbow Strike)

With your right fist clenched, palm up, at the hip and your left arm extended straight out from the body, snap the right elbow up toward your target, turning your hips into the blow, until your fist is at your ear. Retract your left clenched fist to your hip.

OTOSHI HIJI ATE

(Downward Elbow Strike)

With the right hand fully extended above your head—fist clenched—and the left hand extended in front of your body, force your right elbow down onto the target, turning your hips into the blow as you simultaneously return your left clenched fist to the hip. Maximum power can be attained by using the full weight of your body.

USHIRO HIJI ATE

(Rear Elbow Strike)

With you right arm fully extended, fist clenched and palm down, and your left fist clenched at the hip, keep your eyes on the target as you thrust your right elbow back, twisting the wrist so that the palm faces up. Keep your arm as close to the body as possible while executing this technique.

KICKING TECHNIQUES

Kicking requires strength in the hips in order to stand on one leg while executing the kick. Raise your kicking knee high toward your chest and slightly bend the knee of your standing leg for better balance.

MAE GERI KEAGE

(Front Snap Kick)

(1) With both feet together, knees bent slightly and hands out at your sides, (2) raise your right leg up, keeping the foot parallel to the left knee. (3) Snap your leg straight out, extending it fully by hinging it at the knee, and strike with the ball of your foot. Keeping the left foot flat on the floor, (4) return your right foot as quickly as possible.

MAE GERI KEKOMI

(Front Thrust Kick)

(1) With both feet together, knees bent slightly and hands out at your sides, (2) raise the right leg up, keeping the foot parallel to the left knee. (3) Thrust your foot straight out, striking with either the ball of the foot or (3a) the heel. Return to your original position.

APPLICATION

APPLICATION

FUMIKOMI

(Front Stamp Kick)

(1) With both feet together, knees bent slightly and your arms at your sides, (2) raise your right leg as high as possible. (3) Thrust it downward toward your opponent's knee, and strike with the bottom of your foot. Return your leg to position 2 and then to your original position.

Variations of the stamp kick include (A) an outside stamp to the opponent's knee, (B) an inside kick to the knee and (C) a rear stamp to his instep.

APPLICATION

3

B

C

YOKO GERI KEAGE

(Side Snap Kick)

(1) With both feet together, your left fist protecting your solar plexus and your right arm extended, look at your target as you (2) raise your right foot up to your left knee so that the knee of the kicking foot faces the target. (3) Snap the right foot out, hinging at the knee, and strike with the edge of the foot. (4) Retract your foot as quickly as possible.

1

2

3

YOKO GERI KEKOMI

(Side Thrust Kick)

(1) With both feet together, your left fist protecting your solar plexus and your right arm extended, keep your eyes on the target as you (2) raise the right leg up so that the foot is parallel to the left knee. (3) Thrust the right leg sideward, locking it for an instant at the knee and striking with the edge of the foot. Action will be stronger if you turn your hips into the kick.

1

2

4

APPLICATION

APPLICATION

MAWASHI GERI

(Roundhouse Kick)

(1) With both feet together and your arms, fists clenched, extended at your sides, (2) raise the right leg up to your side until it is perpendicular to your body. (3) Turning on the ball of your left foot, execute the roundhouse in a circular motion by turning your hips into the kick. Strike with the ball of the foot by snapping the leg out, keeping the kicking knee as close to the body as possible. Return your leg to position 2 and end in the original position.

1

2

UCHI MAWASHI GERI

(Inside Roundhouse Kick)

(1) With both feet together and your arms, fists clenched, extended at your sides, (2) raise your right leg up and in front of your left leg with the sole of the foot facing upward and the knee facing out at a 45-degree angle. (3) Kick out from and across your own body, striking with the ball of the foot. Return your leg across your body and to your original position.

1

2

3

APPLICATION

3

APPLICATION

USHIRO KEKOMI GERI

(Rear Thrust Kick)

(1) From a ready position with your feet together and fists clenched in front of your body, look at your target (in this case, to the right). (2) Bring your right leg up until the foot is parallel to the left knee. (3) Then thrust out with a back kick, striking with the heel of the foot. Return your leg to position 2 and end in your original position.

USHIRO KEAGE GERI

(Rear Snap Kick)

(1) From a ready position with your feet together and fists clenched in front of your body, look at your target. (2) Snap your right foot up and back. Return to your original position.

APPLICATION

APPLICATION

HIZA GERI

(Knee Kick)

(1) Stand in a ready position with both feet together, knees slightly bent, and your fists clenched at your sides. (2) Keep your left foot flat on the floor as you snap your right knee up, then quickly return your right foot to the floor.

APPLICATION

1

2

BLOCKING TECHNIQUES

Almost any of the blocks described can be interchanged with any stance. Most blocking techniques must be executed with a snapping of the hip.

AGE UKE

(Up Block)

(1) From a forward stance position with your open left hand above your head and your right fist clenched at your hip, (2) lower your left hand to your hip, both hands crossing in front of your body. (3) The movement is completed as you thrust your right, or blocking, hand upward—your fist higher than your elbow—, simultaneously twisting your hip as you return your left hand to your hip.

APPLICATION

3

SOTO UDE UKE

(Outside Forearm Block)

(1) From a forward stance position with your left hand pointed outward, fingers extended, and your right clenched fist held close to your head, (2) begin to snap your left hand toward your hip and at the same time thrust your right forearm forward. (3) The movement is completed as you snap your right hip into the block.

APPLICATION

3

UCHI UDE UKE

(Inside Forearm Block)

(1) From a forward stance position with your open left hand extended over your right arm, right fist clenched, (2) retract your left hand to your hip. (3) The movement is completed as you simultaneously execute an inside forearm block, twisting your hip into the block.

1

2

APPLICATION

JUJI UKE

(X Block Open Hand)

(1) From a cat stance position with both fists at the hips, (2) thrust your hands forward and upward. (3) The movement is completed when your hands cross over your head.

APPLICATION

3

GEDAN BARAI

(Downward Block)

(1) From a forward stance position with your left clenched fist extended and your right clenched fist crossed to the left side of your head, (2) retract your left hand to your hip, simultaneously lowering your right hand in a downward block. (3) The movement is completed as your right hand is extended forward and your left hand returns to your hip.

APPLICATION

3

GEDAN UDE UKE

(Forearm Block)

(1) From a forward stance position with your left hand extended downward and your right hand on your hip, both fists clenched, (2) begin to swing your right hand in front of your body as you retract your left hand to your body. (3) The movement is completed when you swing your arm forward across your body. (Note: Your body must be twisted more than normal to perform this block properly.)

APPLICATION

3

NAGASHI UKE

(Sweeping Block)

(1) From a forward stance position with your left hand fully extended and your open right hand at the side of your head, (2) begin to retract your left hand to your hip as your right hand sweeps in front of your body. (3) The movement is completed by drawing your left hand to your hip as (4) your right hand blocks in front of your body. (Note: This block is executed by sliding the palm of the hand along your opponent's attacking arm.)

APPLICATION

3

4

TEKUBI KAKE UKE

(Wrist Hook Block)

(1) From a *san chin* stance with both clenched fists pointing downward, (2) raise both hands upward, almost crossing each other. (3) The left hand is lifted chest-high as the right hand starts the wrist hook block. (4) The movement is completed as the left hand is retracted to the hip and the right arm is half-way extended forward, palm facing up. (Note: The movement of the right hand is made in a circular motion.)

APPLICATION

3

4

HIJI UKE

(Elbow Block)

(1) From a side stance position with your left hand extended, fist clenched, and right clenched fist at your hip, (2) begin to retract your left hand to your body as you twist counterclockwise. (3) The movement is completed as your left hand returns to your hip and you have snapped your body fully into an elbow block. (Note: If you are squarely facing your opponent, you can apply this block by stepping back on your left foot and continuing as described above.)

APPLICATION

3

SUKUI UKE

(Scooping Block)

(1) From a forward stance position with your open right hand extended slightly toward the right and your clenched left hand straight out, (2) sweep your right hand in front of your body and simultaneously retract your left hand to your hip. (3) The movement is completed as your left hand returns to the hip and your right hand has made a complete sweep across your body.

APPLICATION

3

ALTERNATIVE APPLICATION

The scooping block can also be performed with the opposite hand, as shown above.

SHUTO UKE

(Knife-Hand Block)

(1) From a cat stance position with your open right hand at the left side of your face—palm toward your face—and your open left hand extended, palm down, (2) bring your right hand down forcefully in front of your body with a slight twist of the hand, and withdraw your left hand to your body, twisting the palm up. (3) The movement is completed with the right hand extended out—fingers pointed toward your opponent at shoulder level—and the left hand at solar plexus level.

APPLICATION

3

KO UKE

(Arch Block)

(1) From a cat stance position with your clenched right hand fully extended and your clenched left hand on your hip, (2) lift your right hand upward, fingers pointing down loosely. Snap your wrist upward to block. (3) The movement is completed when the right, or blocking, hand is head-high. The left hand remains stationary at the hip throughout.

APPLICATION

3

SEIRYU TO UKE

(Palm Block)

(1) From a forward stance position with your open right hand held high over your head and your clenched left hand extended forward, (2) withdraw your left hand to your hip as you chop your right knife-hand downward to block. (3) The movement is completed when the right hand is in front of your body and your clenched left hand is at your hip.

APPLICATION

3

MOROTE UKE

(Forearm Block)

(1) From a right forward stance with your clenched left hand on your hip and your clenched right fist extended to the left side of your body, (2) block with your right forearm by thrusting it forward in a circular movement, simultaneously moving your left hand toward your right. (3) The movement is completed with the clenched right fist up, palm facing toward you and the elbow slightly crooked. The right fist is level with the shoulder and the left fist can brace your right elbow against an overpowering attack.

1

2

APPLICATION

3

HAISHU UKE

(Backhand Block)

(1) From a *nai huan chin* (side) stance position with your open right hand crossed under your clenched left fist, (2) block with the back of your right arm as your left hand returns to your hip. (3) The movement is completed when your right hand is aligned with your body and your left hand is retracted to your hip. (Note: If you are squarely facing your opponent, you can apply this block by stepping back on your left foot and continuing as described above.)

APPLICATION

3

AWASE UKE

(Joined Hand Block)

(1) From a cat stance position with your open right and left hands crossed at the wrists, fingers extended upward, (2) snap both hands up to face level to block a face punch. (3) The movement is completed as you move both hands to the side of your head. The use of both hands insures support against an overpowering force.

APPLICATION

3

KAKIWAKE UKE

(Separating Block)

(1) From a cat stance position with both clenched hands fully extended downward, (2) raise your arms to shoulder level, crossing them with palms facing upward. (3) Spread your hands and (4) complete the movement by turning your palms away from you. (Note: This technique can be performed with either open or clenched fists and is a good defense against double-hand reaches and grabs.)

APPLICATION

3

4

KAKETE UKE NAGASHI

(Hook and Sweep Block)

(1) From a *san chin* stance with your clenched left hand facing forward and downward, and your open right hand also facing down, (2) raise both hands in a circular movement. As your hands cross in front of your chest, (3) begin to retract your left hand to your hip. Continue circling your right hand, palm toward you. (4) Turn your palm outward. (5) The movement is completed with the left hand at your hip and the right hand extended, your palm facing away from you.

4

5

APPLICATION

GEDAN JUJI UKE

(Downward X Block)

(1) From a forward stance position with both fists clenched at your hips, palms upward, (2) thrust both hands forward and angling downward, the wrists crossed to jam the kick before it is unleashed. (3) The movement is completed with your hands crossing each other.

APPLICATION

OSAE UKE

(Press Block)

(1) From a cat stance position with your clenched left fist on your hip, extend your open right hand forward, palm facing out. (2) Slap the palm downward to block. (3) The movement is completed with your right hand in front of your chest and your stationary left hand still on your hip.

APPLICATION

3